SEVEN AWFUL THINGS I WANT TO SAY TO DONALD TRUMP

-AND HE WILL REGRET BEING PRESIDENT

BY

DON BERNADATE

.

DEDICATION

To all writers in search of excellence

"Either write something worth reading or do something worth writing."

--Benjamin Franklin

WARNING

If you have a heart condition, do not read beyond this next line. Readers discretion is required for further reading.

Chapter One

THIS IS NOT ABOUT ELECTIONS

I am not a partisan politician. Though I vote in my country, I hold no party card. I also have no sympathy for any of the political persuasions in America. Dogs do not eat grass and do not care how you cook or serve grass. So this is neither about politics nor elections. I only subscribe to politics when time rebrands it as history.

I want to speak some bitter truths. Non-fiction and non-fat pinstripe facts without coloration. Big, black and bold fonts on white magi board needing no spectacles to discern.

I am not the one to beat about the bush. So I will go straight to the point. They say in Africa that a true account does not take the whole night to tell. Therefore, I will be straight specific and short. I vow not to waste your time on semantics.

What do I want to say to Donald Trump? I desperately want a word with President Trump. I guess I should have gone to the White House for this stern talk but wishes are not horses and so beggars do not ride. Much as Mr. Goat desires a gold necklace, it remains a pipe dream because even when and after such a fairy necklace is donated to Mr. Goat, who will put it round his neck? We

do not have friends in the high society.
So we shout where we can.

I know the President deserves some
privacy. Though a public figure, not
everything about him should be public.
He alone, for instance, should know
what he wears underneath daily.

Yet, Donald Trump should get what he
deserves more so harvests of his
vexatious and notorious tweets. I believe
that he deserves to hear from me.

And I wish I could up and knock on
White House doors. However, the road
to the White House is tolled with red
tape, bureaucracy and caution. Truth be
told therefore, I have no doubt that
before I get my golden chance; the huge

head of a Carmel would have passed
through the small eye of the needle a
dozen times.

"Reading is essential for those who seek to rise above the ordinary."

– Jim Rohn

Chapter Two

BUT I WILL NOT THROW IN THE TOWEL

Did Zig Zigler not say when the going gets tough, the tough gets going? They say in Africa that it is for tough situations and circumstances that champion warriors are born.

The situation is excellent: therefore, I speak in public and this serves me well. A monkey, no matter how disappointed, should not kill itself. Rather, he consoles himself with handy bananas. Banana tastes good in the mouth of a monkey, no matter the weather. I know not what you think but some say half loaf is better than none!

Enough of the digressions though. I must hurry off to the point.

Yet, I see my high school logic teacher standing before me. He used to communicate effectively to us by first telling us what the topic is not before homing in to what it is. I guess I should borrow a leaf from him: after all, they say that you do not change a winning formula!

This certainly is not about the four women of color. You have heard enough about their going back to where they came from and all that. No doubt, your ears are full with their responses. They have spoken enough for us to know what they think and what they want to leave unattended to in the matter.

It is not about migrants. It does not matter where the migrants are whether at the Mexican border or somewhere in the moon. Of course, they could be knocking on the doors of Italy or being washed off the shores of Libya for all the man in the White House cares. His tweets are already over-worked. So why add the refugees of Venezuela? The man is too busy to tweet about the refugees of Muslim Rohinger and who wants to offend India over Kashmir? Know you not that the forthcoming elections are internal and not global?

But I digress again.

My talk is not about the raging World War Three. Take it from me: though the weapons of warfare are not bombs, the world is at war. If you doubt that the world is already at war, ask China what hit her currency. Or take a stroll to Wall Street neighbor and ask why everyone is trading with caution. You can also ask the raped banana republics of Africa and Asia why the donor vaults are empty!

But I have to stop here because all the media I see here are CNN and the likes. Will Donald Trump see my message as balanced? All other media I see here are from North Korea, Iran and Venezuela. Should I talk to them? Will the President blink once he knows I am with CNN?

THEY SAID IT

"If all that glitters is gold, then half the story has not been told"

Chapter Three

WELL, I CONFESS

There is another reason why I am stopping now and this is it: for you to read up to this point, I got you. This little book is all about getting people like you to read this far and learn something in the process.

The aim here is to give a brief teaching on: HOW TO WRITE ATTENTION GRABBING TITLES!

Surprised? Well, I warned you at the outset that you will be shocked. So please forgive me. As a medic, I needed to drink my own medicine. Do lawyers not say you cannot give what you do not have?

This is my advice to you: make a gift of this little book to every writer you know. What good is writing a book that no one reads?

The first step to a good book methinks is to craft an attention grabbing title.

The second step in my lay man's mind is to keep the reader guessing what the main point of the book is, till he or she reaches the end of the book.

The third step is......well, you guessed right! Read any of my numerous books and tell somebody about them.

I warn you though, do not read them, if you have a heart condition because some of them will shock but concuss you!

Did I say **concuss?**

Well, that is my fourth step or rule: never make the reader pause and reach out for a dictionary like I have just done. Who has the time?

THANKS FOR READING THROUGH

Please tell me how stupid or otherwise you think this book is.

You can reach me on:

newochei@gmail.com

THESE OTHER BOOKS SHOULD INTEREST YOU

1. FORTY-EIGHT LAWS OF BOOK WRITING
2. HOW TO WRITE TEN THOUSAND WORDS IN A DAY
3. THE REAL MEDICINE PEDDLERS
4. HOW TO KNOW A MAD PASTOR

I THINK I SETTLED ON THE TITLE BEFORE I EVER WROTE THE BOOK

FRANK MCCOURT

https://www.google.com/search?q=QUOTES+ON+BOOK+TITLES&tbm=isch&source=univ&sa=X&ved=2ahUKEwi46qH8i43kAhXxSxUIHVr8BdoQ7Al6BAgGECQ&biw=1280&bih=640#imgrc=DwANmsnrlC1eXM:

NOTES

NOTES

NOTES

NOTES